DIRECTIONS IN

Building Human Capital for Better Lives

George Psacharopoulos

The World Bank
Washington, D.C.

© 1995 The International Bank for Reconstruction
and Development / THE WORLD BANK
1818 H Street, N.W.
Washington, D.C. 20433

All rights reserved
Manufactured in the United States of America
First printing July 1995
Second printing February 1996

This report is a study by the World Bank's staff, and the judgments made
herein do not necessarily reflect the views of the Board of Executive
Directors or of the governments they represent.

ISBN 0-8213-3392-5

Cover photo: Curt Carnemark, World Bank Staff.

This report is the result of a team effort led by George Psacharopoulos,
with major contributions from Joy de Beyer, Diane Steele, Johanna
Coenen, and Fiona Macintosh.

Contents

Foreword

The key words in today's development economics are "human capital." More and more emphasis is being placed on investments in education, health, and nutrition as a means of bettering the lives of people in developing countries. There is now enough theoretical and empirical evidence to indicate that both public and private investments in people contribute significantly to economic growth and the alleviation of poverty. This report examines past advances and current problems in this area of investment and presents the strategies most likely to reduce those problems. It also explains how the World Bank helps countries build human capital.

Beyond what the World Bank can do, governments need to redefine their role in the financing and provision of social services by focusing attention on the selectivity and reallocation of public expenditure toward essential services for the poor. It is also vital to promote decentralization and encourage beneficiaries to participate in the design of programs that affect them. Above all, human capital can only be built within a sound macroeconomic environment.

This short compendium provides in a nutshell the principles on which human capital can be built.

Armeane M. Choksi
Vice President
Human Capital Development
and Operations Policy

1. Building Human Capital

Countries, like individuals, cannot realize their full potential without knowledge and skills, otherwise known as human capital. Investment in education, training, health, nutrition, and other social services is therefore among the most crucial actions needed to achieve rapid, efficient, equitable, and sustainable development.

The importance of investing in human capital has become much clearer in recent years because of the mounting evidence on the extent to which such investment and its links with other factors in development act as an engine of change. So much has been learned, in fact, that the case for increasing emphasis on human capital now needs retelling. The main purpose of this report is to summarize the key arguments in favor of building human capital and to discuss the far-reaching benefits of such activity for developing countries.[1] This chapter briefly explains why building human capital is important, particularly in relation to broader development issues, including economic growth.

Why Building Human Capital Matters

Raising living standards and reducing poverty continue to be top priorities for developing countries and their development partners. The world is approaching the turn of the century with more than 1 billion people living on less than a dollar a day and another 2 billion only marginally better off. These figures could become worse in the decades ahead if economic and social development are not accelerated enough to offset the continued rapid pace of population growth.

But there are also reasons to be hopeful. The past fifty years have seen more progress in improving the human condition than has occurred at any other time in history. Per capita incomes, a measure of average living standards, have more than doubled throughout the world. Life expectancy has gone up from forty to sixty-three years, an increase of more than 50 percent. Infant mortality rates have been cut by two-thirds. The 5 billion people alive today are on average more healthy, better fed, better housed, better educated, and better clothed than all those who lived before them. And with this progress has come an unprecedented hope that absolute poverty, in the sense of severe deprivation of basic needs, may one day actually be eradicated.

Even the strategies needed to achieve further progress in the period ahead have been identified. Compelling evidence indicates that it is crucial to press hard on two fronts simultaneously: stimulate economic growth through sound policies that promote sustainable, equitable development; and invest heavily in human capital through improvements in education, health, nutrition, and other social services.

Both lines of attack must be pursued. Economic growth is needed to generate more opportunities for people to earn their way to a better life. Human capital must be built up so people will have the skills and abilities they need to take advantage of those opportunities. The two reinforce one another. Economic growth—by increasing the demand for labor and the returns to work, through employment, higher wages, and better earnings for small entrepreneurs (including farmers)—makes it more attractive for people to improve their own and their children's skills and abilities and gives them and their governments more resources to do so. Investing in human capital better equips people for new work possibilities and thus makes the entire economy more competitive in global markets and strengthens the prospects for faster economic progress.

The two together can set in motion a "virtuous circle" of mutually reinforcing improvements and thereby break the vicious circle of grinding, binding poverty. But one without the other is not enough. Economic growth will stall if too few people are competent enough to fill new jobs and capitalize on new possibilities. And investing in human capital will fail if too few jobs and opportunities are being generated to make full use of that capital.

Evidence of these phenomena can be found worldwide. East Asian countries emerged from economic despair in the 1950s by investing heavily in human capital in subsequent decades. They also got their economic policies in order. Dazzling progress followed (box 1-1). The industrial countries followed similar paths in earlier centuries. Governments in other parts of the globe are at various stages of applying similar ideas.

**Box 1-1. Education's Contribution to Economic Growth
in East Asia**

Primary education is the largest single contributor to the predicted economic growth rates of high-performing Asian economies. This was the
conclusion reached by a 113-nation survey on the effect of primary school
enrollment and the share of investment in GDP on the rate of real per
capita income growth. (The analysis controlled for the rate of growth of
the economically active population and the gap between per capita income and U.S. per capita income in 1960 at 1980 U.S. dollar prices.) A 10
percent increase in school enrollment was associated with a 0.3 percent
rise in the growth of per capita income.

The high-performing Asian economies showed a significantly faster
rate of growth owing to education than all the other economies in the
study. In a comparison of East Asia and Latin America, 34 percent of the
predicted difference in growth rates could be attributed to higher investment levels and 38 percent to higher enrollment rates. The principal difference between high-performing Asian economies and countries in Sub-
Saharan Africa was due to variations in primary school enrollment rates.
Investment accounted for only 20 percent of the difference and was offset by the more rapid population growth in Sub-Saharan Africa.

Source: World Bank (1993a).

The literature abounds with discussions of the rewards of the two-
pronged strategy. A study of ninety-eight countries shows a strong and
robust positive association between school enrollments and economic
growth rates (Barro 1991). Other studies (such as Psacharopoulos 1984;
Tilak 1989; and World Bank 1993a) tell a similar story. To take but one
example, Pakistan and the Republic of Korea had similar income levels
in 1960, but by 1985 Korea's GDP per capita was nearly three times higher
than Pakistan's, owing in large part to differences in primary school enrollment rates. Fewer than a third of primary school–age children in Pakistan were enrolled in 1960, compared with 94 percent in Korea.

This report focuses on the human capital side of the strategy, for a
great deal has already been said elsewhere about the role of economic
growth in eradicating poverty and about the means of achieving growth
(see, for example, World Bank 1991b). Governments, it is widely argued,
need to curb excessive spending so they no longer run large fiscal defi-
cits and must keep a firm control on inflation, the cruelest of taxes for
the poor. They must also open up trade to external markets through the

elimination of excessive tariffs, quotas, and other restrictive barriers to exports and imports; remove impediments to investment so that external and internal sources of capital can be attracted to productive growth opportunities; and achieve and maintain realistic exchange rates.

In addition, they should dismantle policies that distort incentives, including many controls on prices; correct biases against agriculture; and reduce burdensome regulations and other unnecessary obstacles inhibiting the development of private sector activities in general, and the informal sector in particular. Above all, the composition of public spending needs to be focused on what governments should do, rather than on what can be done better by others, and on what will yield the most benefits to the entire population of a country rather than to an elite few. This means the state should place more emphasis on basic education and primary health and should get out of enterprises that need not be in public hands. Financial intermediaries (such as banks) and legal systems need to become more efficient and effective so that economic agents are not hampered by costly and unreliable disruptions or delays in the flows of funds and the handling of contracts. All these measures will help create and maintain an environment in which growth can take place, and thus human capital investment can yield its highest returns.

How Building Human Capital Helps

Investments in education, health, nutrition, and other social services are of direct benefit to individuals and their families, as well as to society in general. Because of the interrelationships among these different aspects of human capital, investments in each have benefits in others, bringing multiple and mutually reinforcing positive effects.[2]

A SEAMLESS WEB. Through this wide range of benefits, investments in human capital instigate powerful changes in people's lives. Health care and good nutrition improve people's standard of living by reducing sickness and child mortality and by increasing life expectancy. Literacy and numeracy open new worlds, are essential to full participation in modern societies, and make it easier for people to learn new skills throughout their lives. Education is perhaps the single most important variable to affect the health and life expectancy of individuals, because it equips them with the knowledge and the means to choose healthier diets, behaviors, and lifestyles. The improved life expectancy of educated people motivates them to make still further investments in their education and health.

Education and better health interact positively with fertility decisions. Educated men and women tend to choose smaller families and are more likely to use modern contraceptives. As a mother's education and her subsequent earning potential increase, the opportunity cost of having a child rises. Better-educated women marry and start their families later, thereby reducing the health and mortality risks associated with early pregnancies. Surveys in twenty-five countries suggest that if closely spaced births were delayed until mothers wanted them, child mortality could fall 20 percent. Lower infant mortality and increased child survival reinforce parents' decisions to have fewer children. Smaller, well-timed families improve maternal and child health, reduce infant mortality, and enable parents to devote more time and resources to each child. Parents (especially mothers) with at least a primary education are more likely to follow good health, hygiene, and nutrition practices, which will then decrease mortality and morbidity within their families (figure 1-1).

Figure 1-1. Effects of a Mother's Schooling on the Risk of a Child's Death by Age Two, Selected Countries, Late 1980s

Percentage reduction in child mortality

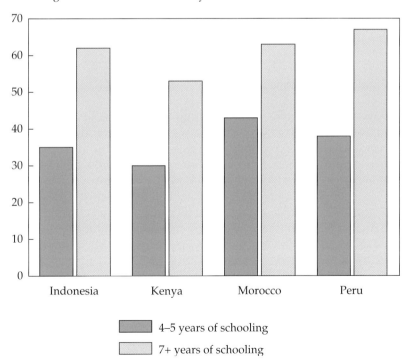

4–5 years of schooling

7+ years of schooling

Note: The percentage reduction pertains to the children of mothers with no schooling.
Source: World Bank (1993c), p. 43.

In short, the positive effects of better health, nutrition, education, and lower fertility are strongly interrelated, and both raise family well-being and prosperity.

The relationship between poverty and human capital investments is clearly evident in countries like Mexico and Brazil, where large pockets of poverty coincide with regional disparities in opportunities for education and investments in health. Because the poor have few physical assets, investing in human capital is often the best way to increase their wealth and access to economic opportunities. The poor, by definition, are unable to invest in themselves. The onus is therefore on the government to see that such investments are made. Although it is impossible to ensure that everyone will receive the same income, the basic health conditions of the majority of people can be improved and equal access to schooling can be provided, at least at the lower levels of education. Since the poor bear a disproportionate part of the burden of disease and malnutrition, investments carefully chosen to improve nutrition and health and make family planning services widely available can have a strong beneficial impact on this group.

REACHING CHILDREN EARLY. Because of the complex connections between the various types of human capital, the early home environment affects the entire course of one's life. Malnutrition and disease are mutually reinforcing, for example, as are health and nutrition, all of which influence early mental and physical development. Malnutrition and the lack of sanitation, health facilities, and other social services are all known to have an adverse effect on the cognitive development of young children living in poverty (Selowsky 1980a; Simmons and Alexander 1980). Early childhood interventions to improve health, education, and nutrition, especially in the first three or four years of a child's life, can have a lasting positive effect (Selowsky 1980b; Halpern 1986; Young 1994). Such measures improve school readiness, which, together with good health and nutrition, increase children's ability and motivation to learn and remain in school. Studies consistently show that malnutrition is related to low cognitive test scores and school performance. Micronutrient malnutrition not only decreases alertness and the capacity to learn, but also increases the chances of becoming blind and can interfere with brain development. Health and nutrition both determine whether children attend school regularly enough to attain a useful level of education and whether they have the mental and physical energy to learn (see box 1-2). With better school attendance and achievement, a child is more likely to complete more years of education.

Box 1-2. The Effect of Malnutrition on Primary School Enrollment

Delayed school enrollment is a pervasive problem in developing countries, despite the fact that it is least costly to send a child to school at the earliest age possible, when the opportunity cost of the child's forgone earnings is at its lowest. Moreover, given that education raises wages, if there is a long delay before a child is sent to be educated, he or she will have less time in the labor market (if retirement ages stay the same) to earn the higher income. The costs of this delay can therefore be substantial.

There are probably several reasons why many people enter school late in spite of the cost of the delay. One relates to the child's nutritional status. Malnutrition plays an important role in the development of a child's physical capacity, cognitive ability, and psychological well-being (Jamison 1986; Leslie and Jamison 1990). Children with severe protein-energy malnutrition in infancy and before school enrollment have been found to perform significantly worse on intelligence tests than well-nourished control children (Pollitt 1984).

A 1988–89 Ghana household survey showed that parents often delay enrolling children who lag behind in their physical development (Glewwe and Jacoby 1993). When controls were used for farm size, father's schooling, income, and caste, the nutritional status of children aged five to eleven in the Terai area of Nepal significantly affected the probability of their being enrolled in school and their progression to higher grades (Moock and Leslie 1986). A study of rural Guatemalan children also found a robust relationship between nutritional status and school enrollment, if other relevant factors were controlled (Balderston and others 1981). In Guatemala and in China, taller children enrolled in school tended to be in higher grades than shorter children of the same age (Jamison 1986).

THE IMPACT OF EDUCATION. Education is strongly correlated with income. A mass of empirical evidence from countries around the world demonstrates that individuals profit from investments in education. Despite the controversies surrounding the mechanisms through which education affects earnings and the methodologies that can be used to estimate the rates of return, the "positive correlation between education and earnings" is "indisputable and universal" (Psacharopoulos 1994). The returns to investments in education tend to follow the same rules as investments in physical capital: that is, they decline as investment is expanded through the educational cycle over time, within countries and across regions. The rate of return is thus highest for primary education, particularly in countries with a dearth of educated workers. Typically, each additional year of education is associated with increases in earnings of 10 percent or more (sometimes up to 20 percent). The jobs that become accessible with education pay more, offer an opportunity for on-the-job training, raise productivity, and bring faster pay increases as work experience accumulates.

Education directly raises productivity in all sectors, in part by increasing the individual's capacity to create and adapt to physical capital, assimilate and efficiently use new input, and cope with other changes (Schultz 1975). In Malaysia, Ghana, and Peru, one additional year of education has been found to increase a farmer's output by 2 to 5 percent, depending on farm size, inputs, hours worked, and other factors. In Thailand, farmers with four years of schooling are three times more likely to adopt new fertilizers and other inputs than farmers with one to three years of schooling (Lau, Jamison, and Louat 1991). As the technologies, processes, and products of modern economies become ever more complex, the premium on education, training, and other sources of knowledge is bound to increase, as is the demand for knowledge and information-based workers (Becker 1994). Some people argue in addition that education is more productive when the state of technology is more volatile (for example, Nelson and Phelps 1966; Welch 1970; and Bowman 1991).

THE IMPACT OF HEALTH AND NUTRITION. Productivity and the length of potential working lives are also directly affected by health and nutrition. Nutritional deficiencies in childhood can affect adult height (which is a good indicator of productivity), morbidity, and mortality (Falkner and Tanner 1986; Martorell and Habicht 1986; Fogel 1990, 1991; Martorell 1993). Weight increases, short of obesity, are also associated with lower mortality (Waaler 1984) and greater productivity as measured by higher wages, particularly at very low levels of calorie intake (Strauss 1986; Behrman 1993). Tea workers in Sri Lanka and cotton mill workers in China whose productivity was adversely affected by iron deficiency experienced a marked increase in work output after taking iron supplements. For most people in developing countries, lost working time because of illness means lost income. In Côte d'Ivoire, the daily wage rates of men who lose a day of work a month because of illness are estimated to be 19 percent lower, on average, than the rates for healthier men. And earnings of lepers in India would more than triple if their deformity could be eliminated.

Survey data suggest that the macroeconomic effects of illness are substantial. The potential income loss from illness in eight developing countries has been calculated at 2.1 to 6.5 percent of yearly earnings whereas the loss in the United States amounts to less than 2 percent.[3] Reducing illness obviously requires resources, but these figures suggest that it might yield a large benefit in economic terms, in addition to the obvious gains for the quality of life (World Bank 1991a).

Mortality reductions may play an important role in promoting economic growth. As adult mortality falls (because of improved health status) and life expectancy increases, people are more inclined to invest in education and training, and these investments, together with lower adult and child mortality, are associated with lower fertility and higher rates of economic growth (as cited in Becker 1995).

FERTILITY. Indeed, fertility choices have great bearing on the relationship between economic growth and human capital investments (Becker 1995). Families choosing to have fewer children are able to invest more in the health, nutrition, education, and training of each. Low fertility, small family size, and large investments in human capital are associated with higher incomes and a faster-growing economy. Better health and lower mortality reinforce these decisions, which lead to a virtuous cycle of prosperity and release individuals from their former trap of poverty, characterized by low investments in human capital, low incomes, high fertility, and low growth. As is widely recognized, rapid population growth can destroy the potential for growth in living standards. Research into the determinants of fertility shows the importance of investments in women.

INVESTING IN WOMEN. Equity reasons and spillover effects on families argue strongly for investing in women. The impact of women's health and education on their childbearing decisions and the health and survival chances of their children, as well as their earning potential and employment opportunities, has already been mentioned (see also Cochrane, Leslie, and O'Hara 1980; Schultz 1993a; Strauss and others 1993). That impact is of enormous magnitude. In Africa, for example, increasing female literacy by 10 percent could lower infant mortality by 10 percent. In India and Kenya, about forty-five infant deaths and two maternal deaths would be averted for every 1,000 girls provided with one extra year of primary schooling (World Bank 1993c). Fewer, better-timed pregnancies substantially reduce the associated mortality risks of childbearing: in Sub-Saharan Africa, where fertility rates still average 6.4, a woman runs a 1 in 22 risk of dying from pregnancy-related causes during her lifetime, compared with a risk of 1 in 10,000 for women in northern Europe. In developing countries, the death of a mother has disastrous consequences for the survival and well-being of her children. In Bangladesh, children whose mothers die are three to ten times more likely to die within two years than those with living parents. In Tanzania, school attendance by children in households where an adult woman has died is only one-half that of their peers.

The equity grounds for more investments in the health and education of girls and women are particularly strong: in the developing world there are 86 females for every 100 males in primary school, 74 in secondary school, and 64 in tertiary education. Women lag in health, too; the differential in life expectancy in most developing countries is much smaller than in industrial countries, where women have a life expectancy more than 1.06 times that of men, and it even drops below that of men in parts of Asia. From infancy, females in many parts of the world not only receive lower-quality and less food, but they get less and later medical treatment when they are sick. In India, protein-energy malnutrition is four to five times more prevalent among girls, and boys are fifty times more likely to be hospitalized for treatment (Dasgupta 1987). In addition to the health and mortality risks of pregnancy, biological factors also make women more susceptible than men to other health problems, including HIV and other sexually transmitted illnesses. Indoor cooking is one of the most serious occupational health and environmental hazards in the developing world because of the consequences of the inhalation of smoke and toxic gases, not to mention accidental burnings. Women's low socioeconomic status, which is reinforced by inferior access to education, can also expose them to physical and sexual abuse and mental depression.

Arguments justifying investments in education, health, family planning, and nutrition can be made on both economic and human grounds. These investments improve equity; improve the well-being of individuals, families, and societies; and promote economic growth. Equally important, they reduce poverty. Tremendous improvements in the key indicators of development have already been made through large investments in human capital around the world. A great deal more remains to be done, however, and many obstacles are yet to be surmounted.

Notes

1. Other related discussions complement the treatment here. See, for example, Summers (1992), Birdsall (1993), and World Bank (1995a, 1995b).

2. For a discussion of the "seamless web" of interrelations among income, nutrition, fertility, education, and health in the development process see World Bank (1980), pp. 68–70.

3. Ghana, Côte d'Ivoire, Mauritania, Indonesia, Philippines, Bolivia, Peru, and Jamaica.

2. The Record So Far and the Priorities Ahead

Great progress has been made over the past fifty years in improving human welfare, the ultimate goal of development. This advance has usually taken place hand in hand with economic growth. Even where growth has lagged, the quality of life has improved. Nevertheless, a number of serious social and economic problems have yet to be resolved, the foremost of which is poverty, particularly the extreme poverty experienced by many indigenous and rural communities. Also of great concern is the self-perpetuating cycle of illiteracy, illness, inadequate nutrition, high fertility, and slow economic growth common in developing countries. As this chapter explains, that cycle can be broken by effective investments in health, nutrition, population, and education. The knowledge needed to guide these investments is now available, as are the technologies needed for implementing them.

Education

Developing countries have already made large investments in education, especially primary education. As a result, enrollments, teachers and schools, and educational attainment have all increased. Between 1980 and 1990 primary school enrollments in all developing countries increased from 69 to 76 percent (table 2-1). East Asia, the Pacific, Latin America, and the Caribbean have had almost universal primary school enrollment for three decades. Countries in South Asia, the Middle East, and North Africa are also making steady progress. South Asia and Sub-Saharan Africa lag, but even there, net primary enrollment has increased, from about 50 percent in 1965 to 70 percent in 1990. Secondary and ter-

Table 2-1. Primary School Enrollment in Developing Countries, 1980 and 1990

(millions)

Population	1980			1990		
aged 6–11	*Total*	*Males*	*Females*	*Total*	*Males*	*Females*
In school	352	198	153	409	220	189
	(69)	(76)	(62)	(76)	(81)	(71)
Out of school	158	64	94	129	52	77
	(31)	(24)	(38)	(24)	(19)	(29)
Total	510	262	247	538	272	266

Note: In keeping with the practice of the U.N. Statistical Office, developing countries are defined here as all countries other than European countries (except the former Yugoslavia), former USSR, Canada, United States, Israel, Japan, South Africa, Australia, and New Zealand. Figures in parentheses are percentages of the total population aged six to eleven in developing countries. These figures do not adjust for countries where primary education begins at age seven and not six.

Source: UNESCO (1993a).

tiary enrollments have increased rapidly, too. Consequently, illiteracy among the adult population dropped from 54 percent in 1970 to 35 percent in 1990 (UNESCO 1990).

In the 1980s, however, enrollment gains slowed markedly, as reflected by a fall in net enrollment ratios (enrollments of children of school age as a proportion of the cohort), particularly in Africa (see table 2-2). About two-thirds of all children who are not attending school can be found in the three regions experiencing the greatest demographic pressures: Africa, with 50 percent of its primary-age children not in school; South Asia, with 27 percent; and the Middle East, with 24 percent.

Many children are unable to attend school because of poverty, their location (usually in remote rural areas), gender, caste, class, ethnicity, religion, and special educational needs. Although the gender gap is now very small in Europe, Central Asia, and Latin America, it remains large in Africa, the Middle East, and South Asia. Of the 130 million primary-age children in developing countries not in school, 60 percent are girls (table 2-1). More than half of all women in developing countries are illiterate, in comparison with 28 percent of the men. Ethnic minorities in addition face linguistic problems that result in higher grade repetition and dropout rates and lower achievement levels. These barriers to schooling affect employment potential and therefore poverty.

Poverty increases child labor, which deprives millions of children in developing countries of education and exposes them to health risks, over-

Table 2-2. Selected Countries with Decreasing Net Primary Enrollment Ratios between 1980 and 1990

(percent)

Country	Net enrollment ratio	
	1980	1990
Sub-Saharan Africa		
Central African Republic	56	56
Guinea-Bissau	60	45
Mali	21	19
Mozambique	36	45
Togo	76	75
United Republic of Tanzania	68	51
Zaire	71	58
Middle East and North Africa		
Iraq	99	94
Jordan	93	91
Morocco	62	57
Latin America and the Caribbean		
Chile	91	87
Colombia	75	74
Costa Rica	89	87
Cuba	95	94
Trinidad and Tobago	89	90
Europe and Central Asia		
Bulgaria	96	84
Greece	96	95
Hungary	95	87
Poland	98	97
Portugal	99	97

Source: UNESCO (1993b).

work, and exploitation.[1] Although most nations have imposed legal restrictions on such labor, these restraints tend to be ineffective because they are inconsistent, contain loopholes, or are weakly enforced. Moreover, the informal sector in which many of the children work is difficult to regulate. The key determinants of child labor are household size and income and schooling opportunities. Financial assistance—such as stipends to compensate families for the loss of a child's labor—may be necessary to enable poor parents to send their children to school.

Between 1980 and 1990 many developing countries recorded an increase in repetition and dropout rates. Students who repeat, especially more than once, are much more likely drop out. At the same time, parents withdraw children from school because of the opportunity costs of their lost labor in the home or income from a job, or because they cannot afford the direct costs of school (the fees, books, and uniforms). Poor-quality education exacerbates dropout and repetition and is a serious problem in itself. Many students in developing countries do not achieve the skills called for in their curricula. Mean levels of achievement in mathematics, science, and reading comprehension are considerably lower than in developed countries.

The quality problems in primary education can be traced in part to declining resource allocations. Such a decline occurred in the 1980s in about half of thirty-seven developing countries for which data are available (UNESCO 1993a). With rising enrollments, quality has suffered in higher education as well. Also during the 1980s, public spending on higher education increased or maintained its share of the gross national product (GNP) in every region except Latin America, yet was unable to keep up with the increasing enrollment rates. Nor is this share optimally allocated, even though education is the largest single item in most public budgets, on average representing 16 percent of government spending in developing countries in 1990.

In many countries, more could be achieved with the same public spending. Experience and research suggest two basic principles for reform and investments in education: redirect more public resources toward primary education, while relying more on private financing at higher levels; and use educational outcomes as the criteria of the effectiveness with which resources are used.

Primary education deserves high priority for four reasons: it is the foundation on which higher education must build; the returns as measured by individual wage gains tend to be largest for primary education (both net and gross of public spending on education); the poor in particular benefit from public spending on primary education; and primary education brings broad additional benefits, ranging from lower mortality and fertility to better health and nutrition and literacy. Widespread literacy helps strengthen all those civil institutions—such as the free press, free elections, unions, political parties, and other representative associations—through which people can participate in the collective decisions that affect their lives. It is far easier to inform a literate population about all sorts of things that promote public or individual interests, such as how to prevent AIDS, cholera, or unscrupulous scams.

In many countries, highly subsidized higher education absorbs much public spending at the expense of primary schooling. This is inequitable, because students in higher education typically come from the highest income groups. It is also wasteful, because the subsidies displace private spending. Increasing the private financing of higher education may be politically unpalatable, but experience from several countries shows that it can be done. Between 1980 and 1990, the share of recurrent higher education costs funded from tuition charges rose from 23 percent to 43 percent in Korea, from 0 to 21 percent in Vietnam, from 13 percent to 25 percent in Mexico, and from 8 percent to 16 percent in Brazil. When coupled with selective scholarships and student loans, tuition increases need not hurt deserving students from low-income families. In most countries, more could be done to encourage private funds to supplement the income of publicly funded institutions or wholly support private schools and universities. This would release public funds and places for more students and would promote diversity and useful competition for public institutions, especially at higher levels of education.

The second principle focuses on outcomes to ensure that children are literate and numerate. That is to say, resources will have been used effectively if their education provides them with knowledge and verbal, computational, communication, and problem-solving skills that can be applied in a wide range of work settings and that will enable people to acquire job-specific skills in the workplace (Becker 1964).

Governments can influence the quality of education in several ways. They need to set clear and high standards of performance in core subjects, and their policies must give schools flexibility and must support inputs known to improve student achievement. Many of these inputs will differ from one country and local situation to another, but five will be important throughout the developing world. First, preschool education programs and preschool and in-school health and nutrition programs will help increase student capacity and motivation to learn. Second, what is to be taught should be defined in curricula and syllabi. At primary levels, considerable attention should be devoted to core skills, which may mean cutting down on the number of subjects. At higher levels, the emphasis should be on "trainability" rather than on job-related skills, which are best taught by employers or private training providers. Third, in-service training, best provided by head teachers or mentor teachers and linked directly to classroom practice, can help improve the teacher's knowledge and repertoire of teaching skills. Fourth, since achievement is directly linked to the amount of learning time, it can be increased by lengthening the school year to permit flexible scheduling to accommodate agricultural seasons, religious holidays, and children's domestic chores and by assigning homework. Fifth, instructional materials—notably blackboards, chalk, and textbooks—are often the most important and cost-effective input for better educational outcomes. Additional books both at home and at school are critical to improving reading skills.

Countries around the world have devised and successfully adopted creative and cost-effective solutions to some of the special problems arising in developing countries. Teacher shortages in rural areas have been eased by recruiting and training teachers in their villages or attracting candidates by providing rural housing or allowances, although the latter solution tends to be much more costly. Another approach, tried in Colombia and Indonesia, has been to ask one individual to teach many grades. Participation in rural communities and student achievement have increased as a result. Correspondence courses offer another cost-effective way of increasing access to education, and radio instruction broadcast directly into classrooms or homes has proved an effective supplemental teaching aid in many countries. Multiple shifts, known as "hot seating" in Zimbabwe, have made it possible to increase enrollment without substantial capital investments. And changes in the design of schools can reduce capital costs without compromising learning or school effectiveness.

Special measures can be introduced to improve access to schooling for the poor, girls, ethnic minorities, and special populations such as nomads and street children. Scholarships and stipends tend to be popular and effective where household financial constraints are binding. Programs for girls feature all-girl schools and classrooms, schools located within easy access of girls' homes, separate and improved sanitary facilities and boundary walls, more female teachers, child care support centers, and flexible school hours to fit girls' work schedules at home or in the fields. In addition, gender or ethnic bias can be reduced in the classroom by making curricula, training materials, teachers, and administrators sensitive to gender issues. Bilingual programs and flexibility in the choice of the language of instruction are important for minority groups, especially in the first years of school.

Furthermore, judicious institutional reform can do much to improve teacher morale and school management, while teaching career ladders, linked to reasonable salary scales, can help schools retain good teachers and improve morale and teaching effort. Management is likely to be much more effective when schools have considerable autonomy and are accountable to parents and communities. Decentralization would enable central educational agencies to concentrate on standards, curricula, and performance assessment and monitoring, and to strengthen information systems that would provide data on student characteristics, school attendance, dropout rates, repetition, teacher qualifications and deployment, and costs. Better data would help guide policies and actions and thereby strengthen the educational system.

Health

Health and life expectancy in the developing world have greatly improved over the past forty years. Smallpox has been eradicated, and vaccines have drastically reduced measles and polio cases. Between 1950 and 1990 the number of children who died before their fifth birthday dropped from 28 in every 100 to 10. Life expectancy in developing countries has risen from forty to sixty-three years, and ranges from fifty to seventy-five, depending on the country income level (figure 2-1). These gains have come from a combination of improved medical technology and expanded medical services, higher incomes, better education and understanding of the causes of disease, and public health measures, especially clean water and sanitation.

Figure 2-1. Trends in Life Expectancy by Demographic Region, 1950–90

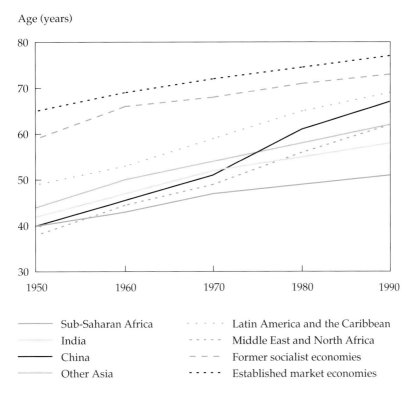

Age (years)

Sub-Saharan Africa
India
China
Other Asia

Latin America and the Caribbean
Middle East and North Africa
Former socialist economies
Established market economies

Source: World Bank (1993c), p. 23.

Despite these advances, disease remains a large burden, much of it preventable or readily treatable. In 1990, 12.4 million children under the age of five died in the developing world. Had they faced the same mortality risks as children in established market economies, this number would have dropped by 90 percent, or 11.3 million. Inadequate diets are implicated in one-quarter of child deaths. Thus even a mild level of vitamin A deficiency increases a child's chances of dying from common infections by more than 20 percent. It costs about $15 in low-income countries to immunize a child fully, and $9 more to prevent and treat diarrheal diseases, acute respiratory infection, measles, and malaria (World Bank 1993c). These investments could prevent nearly half of early childhood deaths in developing countries. Many children who survive are stunted and weakened by malnutrition and disease. Girls are often in poorer health than boys and more girls than boys die before their fifth birthday, despite their innate biological advantage (World Bank 1993c).

Nearly 1 billion people in the developing world lack access to clean water, and 1.7 billion have no sanitation (World Bank 1992). This contributes to 900 million cases of diarrheal diseases each year, which result in more than 3 million child deaths. At any given time, 200 million people are suffering from schistosomiasis or bilharzia and 900 million from hookworm. Water-borne diseases like cholera, typhoid, and paratyphoid remain a pervasive daily threat to health in many developing countries, especially for the poor.

Among adults, communicable diseases continue to be all too common. With the evolution of drug-resistant microbes, malaria and tuberculosis are on the rise and together caused 3 million deaths in 1990. AIDS has emerged as a serious threat and already imposes the highest burden of disease among men between the ages of fifteen and forty-four and is number four for women in the same age group. Sexually transmitted diseases rank second for women in this age group, who face additional risks from pregnancy-related complications and unsafe abortions (World Bank 1993c). The rising per capita consumption of tobacco and alcohol contributes to ill health both directly and through accidents and violence. As populations age, health care systems also have to cope with an increasing burden of noncommunicable problems, such as heart attacks and strokes. These are often difficult and expensive to treat so can absorb considerable health care resources for relatively small health gains.

Developing countries spend about 4 percent of their national income on health. Half of this amount comes from the government. In many countries, better allocation of these resources could increase access to health care and the quality of service, improve equity and health, and save lives. In some regions, especially in South Asia, there are large inequalities in the health status of men and women and their utilization of health services. These disparities could be reduced through family planning, nutritional supplementation, community-based primary health care, and safe motherhood programs (including safe abortion), which tend to have very high health benefits in relation to cost. In addition, health financing and delivery systems could be improved by using generic rather than brand-name drugs and by rationalizing the use of hospital beds and of expensive technology that brings little health benefit in relation to its cost. The poor in particular benefit from investments in cost-effective, preventive, and basic curative health services. Mexico and several countries in the Mahgreb have set about systematically assessing the burden of disease, as measured by the discounted loss of healthy years of life, and the relative cost-effectiveness of different interventions to reduce that burden. This information is being used to guide the reallocation of public expenditures and thus increase health gains (see box 2-1).

Analysis of the "value for money" of different health interventions, measured by the impact on the health of the population, suggests that health policy and expenditure should give high priority to the following four measures:

- Reduce government expenditures on tertiary facilities, specialist training, and interventions that primarily benefit the wealthy and provide few benefits for the cost incurred.
- Strengthen public health interventions that have wide benefits for society and that help the poor in particular, such as infectious disease control, information and selected services for family planning and nutrition, the prevention of AIDS, control of environmental pollution and investments in safe water and sanitation, and regulations to reduce behaviors that put others at risk (such as drunk driving).
- Fund a package of essential clinical services, the comprehensiveness and composition of which will depend on epidemiological conditions, preferences, and income in individual countries.
- Improve the management of public health services, for example, by decentralizing administrative and budgetary authority and contracting out services.

Reform is never easy. Vested interests and inertia are often difficult to overcome. Nevertheless, there are numerous examples from around the world of changes that are being implemented successfully.

Not all health services that are publicly funded need to be provided by the state. Governments can finance care through private providers

---

Box 2-1. Essential Health Services

In a number of cases, health services may have to be provided by the government because there is limited incentive to provide them in the private sector. These services generally include preventive and primary care measures (such as the control and treatment of infectious diseases and malnutrition) and the prevention of AIDS, environmental pollution, and certain risky behaviors such as drunk driving. The more cost-effective items include

- Immunizations
- School-based health services (such as the distribution of micronutrient supplements)
- Information and selected services for family planning and nutrition (such as information on breastfeeding)
- Programs to reduce tobacco and alcohol consumption
- Regulatory action, information, and limited public investments to improve the household environment (clean water, sanitation, garbage collection, public housing)
- AIDS prevention.

The comprehensiveness and composition of the package of essential clinical services will depend on the epidemiological conditions, preferences, and income level of the country in question. At a minimum, six kinds of interventions should be provided:

- Pregnancy-related care
- Family planning services
- Tuberculosis control (mainly through drug therapy)
- Control of sexually transmitted diseases
- Care for the most common serious illnesses affecting young children (notably, diarrheal disease, acute respiratory infection, measles, malaria, and acute malnutrition)
- Some treatment for minor infection and trauma.

The total package would cost approximately US$12 per capita per year in low-income countries (or 3.4 percent of per capita income) and US$22 per capita per year in middle-income countries (or 0.9 percent of per capita income).

Source: World Bank (1993c).

---

and nongovernmental organizations (NGOs). Certainly, governments play an important role in providing policy direction and guidance, promoting efficient and cost-effective approaches, and facilitating private participation in service delivery. Diversity and competition in the financing and delivery of health services can help improve quality, widen choices and access, and lower the public expenditure burden. The state can foster competition among private suppliers of clinical services and inputs such as drugs, and it can encourage the development of private pilot models showing how to manage health facilities. Well-regulated social and private health insurance can increase access to clinical services outside the government's basic package.

Recent reports on access to clean water and sanitation apply these principles in their recommendations (World Bank 1992, 1993b). They suggest that governments switch from a supply-driven water resources strategy to one in which households, both rich and poor, are offered a menu of levels of service priced accordingly. The government would focus on establishing a framework that would facilitate the efficient and accountable provision (often by the private sector) of services that people want and are willing to pay for at full cost, applying graduated fees to assist the poor. In rural areas, and in other instances where people may be willing to pay for services but cannot otherwise afford the high costs of supply, public funds could be used to subsidize provision.

Under this new approach, management and delivery structures would be decentralized, and there would be greater participation by beneficiaries. Many communities in developing countries, with the assistance and encouragement of their governments, are already taking the lead in providing and maintaining local water supplies (World Bank 1991b; Salmen 1992). Because the burden of fetching, bearing, and storing water in these countries usually falls on women, their views must be taken into account in any overhaul of an existing water supply system.

Scientific advances have provided a range of inexpensive clinical treatments and practices that have the potential to achieve further improvements in health and mortality. If their full benefits are to be realized, households must be able to put these advances into practice. Parallel government action is therefore needed to promote market-oriented growth policies that would increase the income of the poor and reduce poverty; increase investment in schooling, particularly for girls; and increase women's economic opportunities and give them legal protection against abuse.

Nutrition

The available data on trends in nutrition in developing countries suggest a general improvement in the past fifteen years, especially in the early part of this period. The percentage of underweight children fell from 42 percent in 1975 to 38 percent in 1980 and 34 percent in 1990

Figure 2-2. Trends in the Prevalence of Underweight Children, 1975–90

Percentage

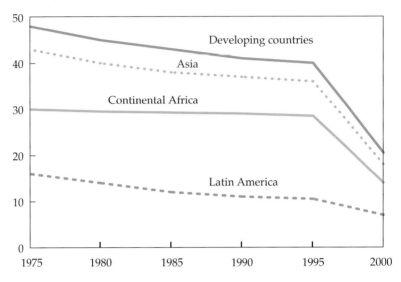

Source: United Nations (1992), p. 13.

(figure 2-2). The proportion of the population underfed—defined as those not consuming enough dietary energy to sustain more than light activity on average—fell substantially, from about one in three people in 1975 to one in five in 1989, leaving fewer people underfed than at any time in the recent past. Even where economic and agricultural conditions have been dire, effective nutrition interventions and advances in knowledge and public education have helped protect nutritional status.

Nutritional gains have been most rapid in the countries of Southeast Asia that have also experienced rapid economic growth and launched vigorous health and nutrition programs at the village level. South Asia has improved more slowly. Latin America and the Caribbean show mixed results: of thirteen countries in which two nutrition surveys were conducted at least two years apart, eight showed declines in malnutrition, despite wrenching economic crisis; in three the incidence of malnutrition was low and fairly stable; and in two others it rose. In contrast to all other regions, nutritional trends in most of Sub-Saharan Africa deteriorated or remained static during the 1980s. One exception was Zimbabwe, where the incidence of malnutrition has fallen even in the face of recurrent and devastating droughts.

Despite these improvements, malnutrition is still prevalent in many parts of the developing world, both because of protein and energy deficiencies and the lack of key vitamins and minerals (known as micronutrients). Either directly or in association with infectious diseases, inadequate diets account for a large share of the world's disease burden, including as much as a quarter of the disease among children. Food consumption is inadequate for an estimated 20 percent of developing country populations. Growth failure affects one-third of children, and in 10 countries more than 20 percent of babies weighed less than 2.5 kilograms at birth, which seriously endangered their health and survival chances. In only 24 of the other 100 countries for which data were available was the percentage of low-birthweight babies below 10 percent. At least 1 billion people around the world are affected by one or more kinds of nutritional deficiency.

Micronutrient deficiencies affect women and children in particular. The biological vulnerability of women, because of the demands of childbearing, is exacerbated in societies where girls are considered less valuable to families and receive less food than boys (Ravindran 1986). An estimated 450 million women are stunted as a result of childhood protein-energy malnutrition (World Bank 1994c). Up to half a million children become blind each year from vitamin A deficiency. About 250 million women suffer the effects of iodine deficiency (Leslie 1991). Furthermore, the lack of iodine is responsible for cretinism in about 6 million people and causes another 20 million to be mentally retarded. Iron deficiency is an even bigger problem. More than half of young children and pregnant women in poor countries are anemic, and this is the one nutrition problem that is growing because of downward trends in dietary iron supply. Iron deficiency saps energy and impairs mental development and performance.

Protein-energy deficiency tends to be poverty related: poor adults simply cannot afford to consume sufficient amounts of food rich in protein and energy. Even so, the protein-energy needs of young children may be met, even in poor families, through behavioral changes such as better hygiene and breastfeeding practices, appropriate weaning, and better understanding of the feeding needs of young children. Micronutrient deficiencies can also be due to poverty, but even as incomes increase, consumers may not necessarily demand micronutrient-rich foods. Therefore, consumers need to be supplied with information about good nutrition and encouraged to adopt healthier diets.

To deal with protein-energy malnutrition in the long term, public sector efforts should be directed at increasing the incomes of the poor. Several strategies can improve nutrition directly and immediately. Early detection, by monitoring and promoting growth in childhood and during pregnancy, makes it possible to treat problems more easily and far more cost-effectively than when malnutrition is full-blown. To be effective, growth monitoring should be combined with food supplementation, nutrition education, and medical referral when needed. The effect of these interventions on malnourished children can be considerable, and the benefits long lasting. Even short-term nutritional deprivation in the early months and years of life can lead to long-term damage, thus influencing the capacity to learn and to grow and eventually to produce.

It is now possible to prevent vitamin and mineral deficiencies for less than one dollar per person per year, which is one of the most extraordinary scientific advances of recent years, with important implications for development. This makes micronutrient programs among the most cost-effective of all interventions (Levin and others 1993; see table 2-3). Deficiencies of vitamin A, iodine, and iron can waste as much as 5 percent of gross domestic product (GDP) in health care costs, missed schooling, and lost productivity, but addressing these deficiencies comprehensively and sustainably would cost less than 0.3 percent of GDP (World Bank 1994b). The problems of iodine deficiency, for example, can be solved by adding iodine to common salt at a cost of about 10¢ per person per year. Similarly, vitamin A can be provided in a variety of forms for about 30¢.

Outside of distributing micronutrients directly, governments can support these efforts by promoting the consumption of micronutrient-rich foods (whether industrially processed or organic). For one thing, they can provide information about the local sources of these foods and can encourage their marketing and production through incentives to industry, such as tax relief, loans for equipment, and subsidies on fortificants. They can also abolish price controls on fortified products such as iodized salt. In some cases, it may also be appropriate to finance or mandate by law micronutrient fortification of certain common foodstuffs or the water supply. In addition, medical personnel should be trained in the prevention and management of micronutrient deficiencies, and pharmaceutical supplements should be aggressively distributed.

Initiating or expanding nutritional programs requires additional resources. A study of nutrition programs in Latin America concluded that adequate nutrition programs would require between 0.5 and 1.5 percent of GDP, depending on country income levels and malnutrition incidence. A large part of this financing could come from shifting resources from ineffective, untargeted food and nutrition programs to expenditures earmarked for poor and nutritionally vulnerable groups. A case in point is Jamaica, where the poorest 40 percent of the population receives only one-third of the benefits of general food subsidies but more than half of

Table 2-3. Cost-effectiveness of Nutrition Investments

Investment	Discounted value of income per program dollar invested[a]
Iron supplements (pregnant women only)	25
Iron fortification	84
Iodine supplements (women of reproductive age only)	14
Iodine supplements (all people under 60)	6
Iodine fortification	28
Vitamin A supplements (children under 5 only)	146
Vitamin A fortification	48

a. The calculations reflect the discounted value of gains in productivity. Calculations of the present value of productivity were based on the following assumptions: life expectancy was assumed to be seventy years; the annual wage rate was assumed to be $500; unemployment 25 percent; the discount rate 3 percent; and coverage and effectiveness of nutrition interventions 75 percent.
Source: Levin and others (1993).

the benefits of food stamps and school feeding. Jordan was able to replace general food subsidies that were costing 3.2 percent of GDP with cash benefits for the poor, while retaining general subsidies on bread and barley, which are the poor's food staples, at less than half the cost, thereby saving 1.8 percent of GDP. A small fraction of those savings could finance a comprehensive micronutrient program.

Who should pay for nutrition programs? Over the long run, with proper information, those who can afford adequate caloric intake would have the knowledge and access to foodstuffs and supplements necessary to avoid nutritional deficiency without subsidy. All donor and government funds could then be targeted to those who cannot afford adequate food. There is good justification for public funding of educational campaigns to build consumer awareness and to cover start-up costs, regulation and monitoring for food fortification, and supplementation. In the short term, subsidies and price regulation may be required to ensure that consumers are not overcharged for enriched foods. As the supplies of a particular foodstuff become fortified and awareness generates a preference for it, the need for price support dwindles.

Population

Thirty years ago, only one couple in ten in developing countries used some form of contraception. That figure has since risen to one couple in

Figure 2-3. Total Fertility Rates by Demographic Region, 1950–95

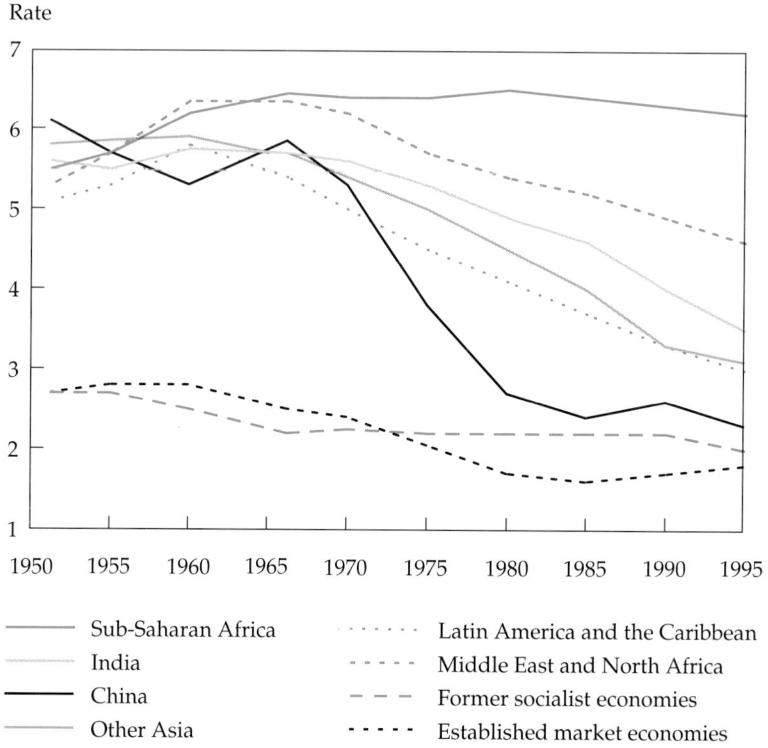
Rate
7
6
5
4
3
2
1
1950
1955
1960
1965
1970
1975
1980
1985
1990
1995
Sub-Saharan Africa
India
China
Other Asia
Latin America and the Caribbean
Middle East and North Africa
Former socialist economies
Established market economies

Source: World Bank (1993c), p. 82.

two. As a result, fertility has dropped sharply: from 6.2 children per woman in 1950–55 to only 3.4 in 1990–95 (United Nations 1993; World Bank 1994a; see also figure 2-3). This change has been fastest in Asia and slowest in Africa. Improvements in health, child mortality, life expectancy, and basic education—especially of women—helped create a demand for smaller families, and the expansion of family planning services and information enabled people to act on those choices.

Despite the sharp drop in fertility rates, the average rate of population growth has decreased much less, from slightly more than 3 percent in the 1950s to just under 2 percent in 1990–95 (United Nations 1993). This decline is due to reductions in child mortality and increases in life expectancy, plus the "population momentum" from the large numbers of couples now of reproductive age who were born before fertility began to decline. Combined with fertility rates that are still well above the replacement rate—the level at which couples have the number of children required to replace themselves (about two)—this will cause a very large increase in absolute population size in the developing regions over the next generation. Between 2000 and 2050, the population of developing countries will grow by nearly 3.5 billion people, an increase of 56 percent, compared with an increase of less than 100 million people, or 7 percent, in the more industrial countries.

High birth rates and very young populations make it more difficult to reduce poverty, invest in human resources, protect the environment, and pursue sustainable economic development. Couples and individuals have the right to decide freely and responsibly on the number and spacing of their children and need the appropriate information and services to enable them to realize their fertility preferences. Opinions differ about the extent to which inadequate family planning services in relation to the demand for large families keep fertility levels above replacement level. There is a consensus, though, that much remains to be done to ensure better access to good-quality family planning, through the prevention and safe management of unwanted pregnancy, as well as to motivate couples to have smaller families. Individual and societal interests can both be served by ensuring that reproductive health services include family planning and are complemented by broader social policies to improve family welfare and reduce poverty. Such policies should include investments in infant and child health, education, and other measures that improve the status of women and remove the legal and regulatory barriers to their full participation in society.

Roughly a quarter of married women in developing countries say they want to space or limit childbirths but are not using any form of contraception. Many other women whose health and lives would be at risk if they had a child do not say that they wish to avoid pregnancy but might if they had adequate information about the risks of a poorly timed pregnancy. These women are potential contraceptors.

Extensive research and field experience have identified the characteristics of effective family planning programs: they provide high-quality care and good access to methods people want, are well managed, involve the private sector, and give clients accurate and ample information.

Access to such services could be increased by offering them in more locations: at all public and private health facilities, pharmacies and stores, or in homes through community-based workers. To do so, it may be necessary to train existing health service providers, deploy more providers in rural and low-income areas, and build partnerships with the private and nonprofit sectors. Effective programs provide a wide choice of methods, along with good information about contraception options and the risks and benefits of each. Providers can be taught to be good counselors, successful motivators, responsive listeners, and competent clinicians. A good-quality service will also be prompt and courteous, will respect the client's privacy and modesty, and be integrated with complementary health services.

Effective programs need strong management to ensure that the system for supplying contraceptives is reliable; that front-line staff receive the necessary training and support; and that monitoring, evaluation, and research are conducted to determine which programs are responding well to local conditions and needs. Effective programs are linked with and support the distribution and promotion of contraceptives by NGOs and other private agencies and practitioners. This effort expands services, relieves the government of administrative and financial burdens, and can lead to program innovations. Before private services can be expanded, regulations that restrict contraceptive use or distribution unnecessarily may have to be changed.

Various means have been used to demonstrate the importance of promoting services widely among the general public as well as among potential and current contraceptive users, family members, and other influential people, including opinion leaders and policymakers, and of providing clients with adequate information on the benefits of spacing and limiting births and effective use of birth control methods. Mass media campaigns can change attitudes and behavior, especially if conducted with skill and tact. Most people support mass media coverage of family planning: at least two-thirds of respondents in national surveys in twenty-two developing countries said they approved of family planning information on radio and television. To be effective, education and communication campaigns must consist of long-term efforts to change attitudes and behavior and sustain the changes.

Family planning programs cost between $1 and $2 per capita per year in developing countries, or about $10–$25 per contraceptive user per year. This is a modest sum compared with the costs of antenatal and postnatal care and education. The total resources needed to provide services to the increasing numbers of couples of reproductive age and currently underserved groups are considerable. Expenditures on family planning services would have to expand by at least 55 percent over the 1990s, and perhaps double or triple in order fully to meet family planning needs as well as broader reproductive health services (World Bank 1993c; UNFPA 1994). The estimates are imprecise partly because recurrent costs and the capital investments needed vary greatly from one country to another.

Public financing and service provision should focus on underserved groups, especially the poor. In some countries, more private sector provision of services to higher-income clients and some cost recovery could free resources to expand information and services for the poor. The poorest countries may need to rely on donor funds to help cover shortfalls in government and client resources, but most programs should rely less on donors and more on government and user financing as they mature, to ensure sustainability.

Note

1. Most child labor can be found in Asia and Africa, which together account for more than 90 percent of total child employment (ILO 1993). India has 44 million child laborers, giving it the largest work force in the world. In Pakistan, 10 percent of all workers are between the ages of ten and fourteen (Weiner 1991). Nigeria has 12 million child workers. Child labor is also common in South America. For example, there are 7 million children working in Brazil (ILO 1992).

3. Next Steps

As governments throughout the world are discovering, it is possible to "cluster" human capital investments to take advantage of the positive cross-sectoral effects discussed in chapter 1. For example, school meals or snacks deliver nutrition along with education, and many countries have begun delivering health services such as deworming, hearing tests, and growth monitoring to children at school, to take advantage of their accessibility and the assistance of school staff.

Opportunities for Clustering

Two outcome-oriented, cross-sectoral initiatives are described here: early childhood development programs, which are growing in popularity in the wake of mounting evidence of their effect on realizing human potential; and the integration of family planning services with broader reproductive, maternal, and child health care, which is becoming standard practice in the developing world.

Multisectoral Approaches to Early Childhood Development

Research indicates that the early years of life are critical to the formation and development of intelligence, personality, and social behavior. By the time a child is four or five, major developmental patterns are already set. Inadequate intellectual stimulation coupled with malnutrition or other physical deprivation during this time can irreparably damage a child's capacity to learn, grow, and eventually produce and reproduce. Early investments in childhood development not only improve the life and potential of a child but also have many social benefits.

All the various needs of a child can best be met through an integrated package of health, nutrition, and educational interventions. There are numerous opportunities to intervene in cost-effective ways. Contrary to common belief, malnutrition of the very young child rarely reflects a lack of food in the home. More often, it is a product of the feeding practices, childcare practices, and the health environment to which the child is exposed (Young 1994). Critical interventions include prenatal care to prevent low birthweights (which start the downward spiral), followed by programs that encourage breastfeeding, improve the way children are weaned, and inform parents and caregivers about the special feeding needs of young children. They also help reduce the frequency of common illnesses by promoting better hygiene and detecting growth failure early.[1] Since malnutrition and disease are mutually reinforcing, the combined effect of these interventions is greater than the sum of their parts.

In addition to the foregoing services, infants and young children need social and intellectual stimulation. Many of the children entering primary school are ill-equipped to learn and therefore are more likely to repeat a grade or eventually drop out. There is ample evidence to indicate that well-designed and implemented early childhood development programs more than pay for themselves in the long run by increasing the efficiency of investments in primary and secondary education, contributing to the child's future productivity and income, and reducing the costs of social services (Barnett 1992). Childcare programs can also stimulate community development and free siblings to attend school and mothers to take jobs.

Several channels can be used to improve child development, beginning with parents themselves and other caregivers, both of whom can be provided with information and training. Some services can be delivered directly to children, whereas others can be provided indirectly, by promoting community development as a basis for the social and political change required to improve conditions that affect child development, by increasing public awareness of and demand for early childhood services, and by strengthening the institutions that provide them (see table 3-1). Nonformal channels have proved affordable and effective; box 3-1 gives two examples of programs assisted by the World Bank.

Multisectoral Approaches to Reducing Fertility

A study of government policies affecting fertility in Sub-Saharan Africa has shown that fertility has declined most rapidly in countries that have

Table 3-1. Early Childhood Care and Development: Program Strategies

Participants and beneficiaries	Objectives	Models and examples
The child: 0–2 years and 3–6	Survival Comprehensive development Socializaion Improvement of child-care	Home day care (Colombia, Bolivia) Integrated child development centers (India, Brazil) "Add-on" centers (Ghana, Senegal) Preschools (formal and non-formal) (Peru)
Parents, family Siblings Public	Create awareness Change attitudes Improve or change practices	Home visiting (Indonesia, Peru) Parental education (China) Child-to-child programs (Jamaica, Chile)
Community Leaders Promoters	Create awareness Mobilize for actions Change conditions	Technical mobilization (Malaysia) Social mobilization (Thailand)
Program personnel professionals, paraprofessionals	Create awareness Improve skills Increase material	Training (Kenya) Experimental demonstration projects Strengthening of infrastructure
Policymakers Public Professionals	Create awareness Build political will Increase demand Change attitudes	Social marketing (Jamaica) Knowledge dissemination (Nigeria)
Working women with young children Working children	Increase awareness of rights and legal resources Increase use of ILO legislation Increase monitoring and compliance with international conventions	Workplace (Brazil) Day care facilities Protective environmental standards (India) Maternal leave and benefits (Colombia) Support breastfeeding by working mothers
Families with young children	Encourage family-sensitive employ-ment practices	Innovative, joint public/private arrangements (India, Colombia) Tax incentives for formal, quasi-formal private enterprises

Source: Young (1994).

Box 3-1. Examples of Early Childhood Development Projects

Delivering services to children in Bolivia

The Bolivian Integrated Child Development Project supports the development of almost 9,000 day-care centers to provide nonformal, home-based, integrated child development services to more than 200,000 impoverished children six months to six years of age. Caregivers from the community are selected and receive credit to finance the rehabilitation of their home, which serves as the day-care center. There the children receive nutritional supplements, a basic package of education services, and, through agreements with local health centers, access to key preventive and curative health care. The typical center operates forty hours a week, twelve months a year. Parents pay US$2.25 a month per child. Colombia has a similar program.

Educating caregivers in Mexico

About 12,000 community educators in poor, rural, and marginal urban areas in ten targeted states (the poorest, with the worst education indicators, and with the largest indigenous populations) meet weekly with parents and hold periodic group meetings. They train and motivate parents to provide richer learning environments for their young children, using illustrated guidebooks and other materials. The community educators are also trained in health, hygiene, nutrition, and family planning, to help serve a wide range of family needs. The program is expected to reach 1.2 million children and indirectly benefit 2 million siblings.

Source: Young (1994).

---

adopted multisectoral approaches to family planning, linking it with girls' education, child and maternal health, and a move to extend property and other rights to women.

Although the use of contraceptives is the direct way to reduce fertility, the factors that induce people to adopt this practice are the true causes of fertility reduction. It is particularly important to invest in the education of girls, because there is overwhelming evidence that birth rates and contraceptive use are closely linked to women's education. Increases in female educational attainment and male and female wages were responsible for about 90 percent of the increase in contraceptive use in Indonesia from 1982 to 1986 (Gertler and Molyneaux 1993; see table 3-2). Although the increased use of contraception accounted for 75 percent of the actual fertility decline, the rise in female education was responsible for 54 percent of the increase in contraceptive use. Girls educated in the 1960s and 1970s who were bearing children in the 1980s were able to take advantage of the good family planning services developed during the 1970s. Female education was also found to be the dominant factor in fertility declines in a cross-country analysis (Schultz 1993b). In Kenya, only 15 percent of married women with no formal education use contraception, whereas 45 percent of those with at least a minimum of secondary education do so (NCPD 1993).

Education can only have this great an impact under a highly responsive contraceptive delivery system (Gertler and Molyneaux 1993). Similar results may not occur if access to these services is limited, whether because of resource constraints, the lack of a political will to provide the services, or regulations that prohibit the private sector from providing them. Even where services exist, they may not be much used if they are of poor quality, the choice of methods is limited, or the costs of the service are too high.

Community-based services that integrate family planning, mother and child care (which includes nutrition education and supplementation), and primary health care are highly effective because they are readily accessible, address a wide range of women's needs, and save women time. Community-based outreach can be a cost-effective complement to facility-based primary health care systems, particularly if these systems are underused for reasons of inaccessibility. Within integrated programs, specific interventions such as the distribution of iron folate tablets, iodine fortification, and targeted calorie supplements to adolescent girls and women of reproductive age and to malnourished pregnant women can add years of healthy life to mothers and children at a low cost. Furthermore, each contact between a client and community health workers in such a programs offers an additional opportunity for motivating couples to space or limit their families.

Women are also more likely to use family planning services offered in the context of care for their overall reproductive and other health needs. Indeed, advocates of reproductive rights consider it unethical to promote family planning specifically and primarily to reduce population growth, arguing that family planning *must* be offered in the context of reproductive health services. The Safe Motherhood Initiative launched in 1987 by governments, donors, and local agencies includes a wide range of measures for improving women's health status: family planning services, prenatal and postpartum care, training and deployment of midwives, and treatment for risk factors such as anemia, hypertension, and sexually transmitted diseases. This initiative has been particularly effective in reducing maternal mortality rates because it takes a strategic ap-

Table 3-2. Sources of Fertility Decline in Indonesia, 1982–86

(percent)

Source	Contribution to fertility reduction
Rise in contraceptive use	
Increase in women's education	54
Higher wages for men and women	36
Spread of family planning services	6
Other factors	4
All factors	100
Proximate source	
Rise in contraceptive use	75
Delayed age at marriage	17
Other factors	8
All factors	100

Note: Between 1981–84 and 1983–87, Indonesia's total fertility rate fell from 4.1 births per woman to 3.4. On Java-Bali, it fell from 3.7 to 3.2.

Source: Based on Gertler and Molyneaux (1993), tables 2 and 8.

proach to the issue, beginning with good nutrition for adolescent girls and continuing with information and education about reproductive health.

Issues

Several other issues need to be addressed as well before a nation can hope to proceed successfully with its plans for human resource investment. Perhaps most important, it must decide what role the government is to take. Attention must also be given to the technical capacity of the implementing agencies and the system of data collection and analysis.

The Government's Role

The appropriate role of the government in building human resources will, of course, vary from country to country. It will depend on income levels, existing institutions, a country's priorities, and the nature of the implicit social contract or explicit political promises. In the extensive debate on this subject, experts have come to agree that three guiding principles must be observed to make the most of limited resources for human capital investments.

REDEFINE THE ROLE OF GOVERNMENT AND BE SELECTIVE. Governments and the private sector have complementary roles to play in the development of human resources. Governments must decide what services they can and should finance, and which ones they should provide directly. It makes sense for them to concentrate on services that generate the highest social benefits, have the broadest positive cross-sectoral effects, are the most cost-effective, and are undersupplied by the private market. Typically, their role will be to provide information that will enable individuals to make informed choices in consuming services; to finance goods and services with large externalities or spillover benefits, such as immunizations, vector control, and basic education; and to provide services that reduce poverty, such as basic clinical health care, education, and nutritional services. In many countries, government regulations could be modified to widen the scope for the private provision and financing of education and health services. Most developing countries would have to undergo major changes, however, to move toward a system in which the government's role is to create an enabling environment for the private sector, regulate where necessary, and deliver key public services.

REALLOCATE PUBLIC EXPENDITURES TO CONCENTRATE ON ESSENTIAL SERVICES AND THE POOR. Most governments operate under considerable resource constraints while facing a growing demand for social services, all of which forces them to be highly selective in their choices. One way to address this problem is to decide which human capital investments are essential for realizing human potential and ensure that everyone has access to the services involved. These essentials might include basic education, public health, and selected clinical services (such as family planning and protection against poverty-related nutritional deficiencies). Governments should also target services to poor citizens who cannot afford to obtain them privately. In most developing countries, existing resource constraints still leave enough room to reallocate public expenditures away from activities that the private sector can undertake, from military expenditures, and from activities, such as tertiary hospital care or a university education, that many beneficiaries could afford themselves, whether out of pocket or through insurance, loans, or scholarships. For example, expenditures could be reallocated from generalized to targeted subsidies, from higher to primary education, and from specialized, tertiary health facilities to public health interventions. Despite the opposition to such changes from those with a vested interest in the current system or with a political axe to grind, many governments have been able to build support and effectively implement clearly justified reforms.

DECENTRALIZE AND INCREASE PARTICIPATION. As many countries have already learned, excessive centralization of the agencies of government overloads their staffs and channels investments into programs that do not meet the needs of the ultimate beneficiaries well. To increase program effectiveness, it may be necessary to decentralize control over some or all aspects of the intervention, whether control moves down within the ministry or is transferred to local governments, community groups, or NGOs. Broader participation by these groups, especially direct stakeholders, can improve a program's impact, not to mention the efficiency of its operations. Decentralization can reduce the burden on the central government and take advantage of participants' knowledge of local conditions, which in turn will make it easier to identify and reach specific groups, as well as spread information about the program's services. If decentralization is to succeed, local institutions may have to be strengthened and a concerted effort made to avoid concentrating power in the hands of the local elites who may be resistant to change. Clearly, the pace and scope of decentralization must be tailored to the circumstances of individual countries. Participation that gives local people and beneficiaries a strong say in the services that affect their lives makes those services more responsive to their needs and can increase cost-effectiveness. Where practical, subsidies provided directly to beneficiaries rather than indirectly to providers will prevent benefits from leaking out to those who do not qualify and will increase coverage of the intended beneficiaries.

Implementing Agency Capacity

Ministries and other public sector organizations cannot build human resources as expected without the requisite technical skills. Moreover, an underpaid and overmanned civil service will only reduce effectiveness and morale. A number of countries, especially in Africa and Latin America, have devised programs to downsize their government while strengthening its capacity. Many have strengthened personnel management, in part by introducing comprehensive management information systems and revising the civil service code to introduce merit-based recruitment and promotion, incentive-based compensation, and clearly defined, reward-oriented career paths.

Many countries must also contend with inadequate accounting procedures and poor financial accountability. The challenge for them is to introduce transparent budgeting systems, improve their accounting and auditing practices, and bring about better compliance with financial management standards. Financial efficiency cannot be achieved unless public financing of social services is based on the actual services provided, rather than on budget allocations of the past.

Data and Analysis

A government can neither design effective policies and programs nor evaluate their impact without up-to-date and accurate data on the social sectors. Furthermore, it must have the capacity to analyze such data quickly. Existing methods of collecting information in many cases fall short of producing the necessary inputs for effective policymaking and planning. To fill these gaps, a growing number of countries are conducting household surveys, often with donor support. Surveys that have been tested elsewhere can be adapted, can be repeated regularly to generate comparative data over time, and can capture some of the interrelationships among sectors. Household surveys are also becoming easier to carry out with the modern information technologies, which permit more rapid data entry and management and, consequently, a fast turnaround between the completion of fieldwork and the production of the final data. International experience with smaller, quicker, cheaper, and more narrowly focused surveys is also expanding. These are designed to monitor poverty or malnutrition or the impact of a particular policy or program, and can be integrated with other methods of collecting data, such as focus group interviews.

Once data are collected and processed, it is important that they be used to analyze the impact of policies and programs on the poor or other groups in the population. A good number of government statistical agencies and sectoral ministries lack the resources to analyze data quickly and fully. A government can enhance its own efforts by making survey data widely available to the private sector—universities, research institutes, trade unions, professional associations, and grass roots groups—and donors. Donors and local agencies can work together to build analytic capacity in NGOs, other institutions within the country, and within the government.

The World Bank's Role

Reducing poverty and improving living standards in the developing world is at the core of the World Bank's mandate. The means to this end is sustainable economic growth and investment in human capital. That is to say, poverty can only be reduced once a country enters upon a path of efficient, long-term growth. That will enable it to make effective use of the skills of the poor and at the same time ensure that this segment of

Figure 3-1. Trends in World Bank Lending for Human Resources

Average annual commitments (millions of U.S. dollars)

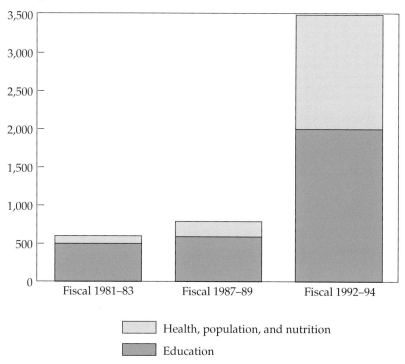

Health, population, and nutrition

Education

Source: World Bank data.

the population is healthy and capable of responding to labor market opportunities.

The World Bank has greatly increased its role in the social sectors because of the strong, multiple, and interrelated benefits of investing in education, health care, family planning, and nutrition, as summarized in chapter 1. Although much has been achieved as a result of these efforts, a great many challenges and opportunities for investment remain that are likely to have large payoffs in human and economic terms. Since the first loan to support human capital investments in 1962, the Bank has lent $28 billion to 110 countries for education, health, population, and nutrition programs. Annual lending for the social sectors has steadily increased, especially over the past fifteen years. Since the early 1980s, borrowers' demand for Bank support for human capital investments has risen rapidly, and annual Bank lending for human resources has more than tripled since 1981 (figure 3-1).

Figure 3-2. Human Resource Lending as a Percentage of All World Bank Lending

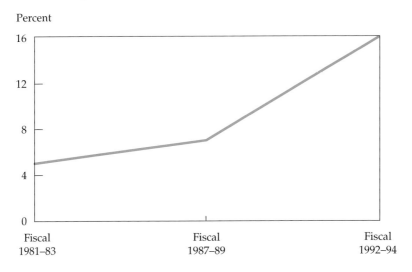

Percent

Source: World Bank data.

The World Bank is today the largest single source of external finance for education, health, and nutrition and for certain specific activities, notably programs to combat AIDS, for which Bank lending so far amounts to $600 million. New lending each year is now in the neighborhood of $2 billion for education, $1 billion for health, $150 million for population, and $180 million for nutrition activities. Together, the share of these sectors in total Bank lending has risen from about 5 percent in the early 1980s to 15 percent in 1992–94 and is expected to continue to grow, to $15 billion over the next three years (figure 3-2). The composition of this lending has been changing, with more emphasis being given to primary education, girls' education, and primary health care (figure 3-3).

In its policy advice and technical assistance to countries, the Bank emphasizes investments in people, and macroeconomic and sectoral policy reform packages now routinely include measures to protect and increase public expenditure on primary education and essential health services. The Bank also places great emphasis on working with developing countries to help them make better investments in human development. To do that well, the Bank must continually improve its operations.

Figure 3-3. Growth of the Share of World Bank Education Lending for Primary Education

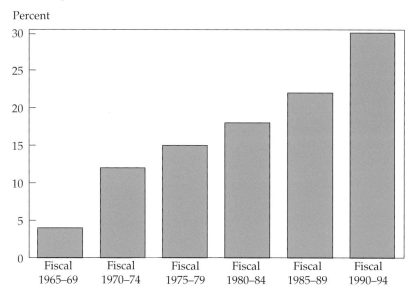

Percent

| Fiscal 1965–69 | Fiscal 1970–74 | Fiscal 1975–79 | Fiscal 1980–84 | Fiscal 1985–89 | Fiscal 1990–94 |

Source: World Bank data.

Three main themes have emerged from the lessons of recent experience. First, new efforts are under way to concentrate resources on services that will have the greatest impact and generate the most benefits in relation to costs. Second, resource allocations will obtain their direction from listening to, learning from, and working with communities and households, for they are the crucial participants in and beneficiaries of human resource investments. Third, the Bank is seeking fresh ways of using collaboration—partnership—among all interested parties to move toward common goals.

Although the precise approach taken to human resource development has to be country-specific if interventions are to be appropriate, feasible, and sustainable, the sectoral and cross-sectoral policies outlined in this volume have a proven record of success in developing countries.[2] However it is done, investing in people is a vital prerequisite for reducing poverty and sustaining economic growth in developing countries. The goal of economic and social development is, after all, to improve the lives of people everywhere—by alleviating widespread poverty, spreading opportunities for more productive work, and pulling societies together for the equitable and participatory advancement of common purposes.

Notes

1. According to the World Health Organization, the deaths of more than a million infants a year could be prevented if all babies were exclusively breastfed for four to six months.

2. Seventeen examples from around the developing world are included in World Bank (1995b).

Bibliography

Balderston, L. B., A. B. Wilson, M. E. Freire, and M. S. Simenon. 1981. *Malnourished Children of the Rural Poor—The Web of Food, Health, Education, Fertility and Agricultural Production.* Boston: Auburn House.

Barnett, W. S. 1992. "Benefits of Compensatory Pre-school Education." *Journal of Human Resources* 27: 2.

Barro, R. J. 1991. "Economic Growth in a Cross-section of Countries." *Quarterly Journal of Economics* 106 (May): 407–43.

Becker, G. S. 1964. *Human Capital: A Theoretical and Empirical Analysis, with Special Reference to Education.* New York: National Bureau of Economic Research.

———. 1995. "Human Capital and Poverty Alleviation." HRO Working Paper 1. World Bank, Office of the Vice President Human Resources Development and Operations Policy, Washington, D.C.

Behrman, J. R. 1993. "The Economic Rationale for Investing in Nutrition in Developing Countries." *World Development* 21 (11): 1749–71.

Birdsall, Nancy. 1993. *Social Development Is Economic Development.* HRO Working Paper 1. World Bank, Office of the Vice President Human Resources Development and Operations Policy, Washington, D.C.

Bowman, M. J. 1991. "Educational Inequalities and Opportunity in Economic Perspective." *Oxford Review of Education* (Spring): 111–37.

Carvalho, Soniya. 1994. "Social Funds: Guidelines for Design and Implementation." HRO Working Paper 34, World Bank, Office of the Vice President Human Resources Development and Operations Policy, Washington, D.C.

Chen, S., G. Datt, and M. Ravallion. 1993. *Is Poverty Increasing in the Developing World?* World Bank Policy Research Working Paper 1146. Washington, D.C.

Cochrane, Susan H., Joanne Leslie, and D. J. O'Hara. 1980. *The Effects of Education on Health.* World Bank Staff Working Paper 405. Washington, D.C.

Dasgupta, M. 1987. "Selective Discrimination against Female Children in Rural Punjab, India." *Population and Development Review* 13 (1): 77–100.

Falkner, F., and J. M. Tanner, eds. 1986. *Human Growth: A Comprehensive Treatise.* Vol. 3. 2d ed. New York: Plenum Press.

Fogel, R. 1990. "The Conquest of High Mortality and Hunger in Europe and America." National Bureau of Economic Research Working Paper 16. Cambridge, Mass.

————. 1991. "New Sources and New Techniques for the Study of Secular Trends in Nutritional Status, Health Mortality and the Process of Aging." National Bureau of Economic Research Working Paper 26. Cambridge, Mass.

Gertler, P., and J. Molyneaux. 1993. "How Economic Development and Family Planning Programs Combined to Reduce Indonesian Fertility." Labor and Population Program Working Paper 93-08. RAND, Santa Monica, Calif.

Glewwe, Paul, and Hanan Jacoby. 1993. *Delayed Primary School Enrollment and Childhood Malnutrition in Ghana: An Economic Analysis.* World Bank Living Standards Measurement Study Working Paper 98. Washington, D.C.

Haddad, Wadi D., Martin Carnoy, Rosemary Rinaldi, and Omporn Regel. 1990. *Education and Development: Evidence for New Priorities.* World Bank Discussion Paper 95. Washington, D.C.

Halpern, R. 1986. "Effects of Early Childhood Intervention on Primary School Progress in Latin America." *Comparative Education Review* 30 (2): 193–215.

International Labour Office (ILO). 1992. *World Labour Report 1992.* Geneva.

————. 1993. *Bulletin of Labour Statistics 1993–3.* Geneva.

Jamison, Dean T. 1986. "Child Malnutrition and School Retardation in China." *Journal of Development Economics* 20.

Lau, L. J., Dean T. Jamison, and F. F. Louat. 1991. "Education and Productivity in Developing Countries: An Aggregate Production Function Approach." Welfare and Human Resources Division Policy Research Working Paper 612. World Bank, Population and Human Resources Department, Washington, D.C.

Lau, L. J., Dean T. Jamison, S.-C. Liu, and S. Rivkin. 1993. "Education and Economic Growth: Some Cross-Sectional Evidence from Brazil." *Journal of Development Economics* 41: 45–70.

Leslie, Joanne. 1991. "Women's Nutrition: The Key to Improving Family Health in Developing Countries?" *Health Policy and Planning* 6 (1): 1–19.

Leslie, Joanne, and Dean T. Jamison. 1990. "Health and Nutrition Consideration in Education Planning. 1. Educational Consequences of Health Problems among School-Age Children." *Food and Nutrition Bulletin* 12 (3): 191–203.

Levin, H. M., Ernesto Pollitt, R. Galloway, and J. McGuire. 1993. "Micronutrient Deficiency Disorders." In Dean T. Jamison and W. Henry Mosley with others, eds., *Disease Control Priorities in Developing Countries.* New York: Oxford University Press.

Lockheed, Marlaine E., Adriaan M. Verspoor, and associates. 1991. *Improving Primary Education in Developing Countries.* New York: Oxford University Press.

Martorell, R. 1993. "Enhancing Human Potential in Guatemalan Adults through Improved Nutrition in Early Childhood." *Nutrition Today*: 6–14.

Martorell, R., and J. P. Habicht. 1986. "Growth in Early Childhood in Developing Countries." In F. Falkner and J. M. Tanner, eds., *Human Growth.* Vol. 3. New York: Plenum Press.

Moock, Peter R., and Joanne Leslie. 1986. "Childhood Malnutrition and School-ing in the Terai Region of Nepal." *Journal of Development Economics* 20: 33–52.

National Council for Population and Development (NCPD), Central Bureau of Statistics and Macro International. 1993. *Kenya's Demographic and Health Survey 1993.* Nairobi.

Nelson, R. R., and E. S. Phelps. 1966. "Investment in Humans, Technological Diffusion, and Economic Growth." *American Economic Review* 65: 69–75.

Patrinos, H. A., and George Psacharopoulos. 1995. "Educational Performance and Child Labor in Paraguay." *Educational Development* 15 (1): 47–60.

Pollitt, Ernesto. 1984. "Nutrition and Educational Achievement." Nutrition Education Series, Issue 9. ED-84/WS/66. UNESCO, Paris.

Pollitt, Ernesto, P. Hathirat, N. J. Kotchabhakdi, L. Missell, and A. Valyasevi. 1989. "Iron Deficiency and Educational Achievement in Thailand." *American Journal of Clinical Nutrition* 50: 687–97.

Psacharopoulos, George. 1984. "The Contribution of Education to Economic Growth: International Comparisons." In J. W. Kendrick, ed., *International Comparisons of Productivity and Causes of the Slowdown.* Cambridge, Mass.: Ballinger.

———. 1994. "Returns to Investment in Education: A Global Update." *World Development* (September).

Psacharopoulos, George, and H. A. Patrinos, eds. 1994. *Indigenous People and Poverty in Latin America: An Empirical Analysis.* Washington, D.C.: World Bank.

Ravindran, Sundari. 1986. *Health Implications of Sex Discrimination in Childhood.* WHO/UNICEF/FHE 86.2. Geneva.

Rosenzweig, M. R., and T. P. Schultz. 1983. "Consumer Demand and Household Production: The Relationship between Fertility and Child Mortality." Discussion Paper 436. Yale University, Economic Growth Center, New Haven, Conn.

Salmen, Lawrence F. 1992. *Reducing Poverty: An Institutional Perspective.* World Bank Poverty and Social Policy Series Paper 1. Washington, D.C.

Schultz, T. P. 1993a. "Demand for Children in Low-Income Countries." In M. R. Rosenzweig and O. Stark, eds., *Handbook of Population and Family Economics.* Amsterdam, N.Y.: North-Holland Press.

———. 1993b. "Sources of Fertility Decline in Modern Economic Growth: Is Aggregate Evidence on the Demographic Transition Credible?" Working Paper 58. Institute for Policy Reform, Washington, D.C.

Schultz, T. W. 1975. "The Value of the Ability to Deal with Disequilibria." *Journal of Economic Literature* 13: 827–46.

Selowsky, Marcelo. 1980a. "Nutrition, Health and Education: The Economic Significance of Complementarities at Early Ages." In P. Streeten and H. Meier, eds., *Human Resources, Employment and Development.* Vol. 2. New York: St. Martin's Press.

———. 1980b. "Preschool Age Investment in Human Capital." In J. Simmons, ed., *The Education Dilemma.* Oxford: Pergamon Press.

Simmons, J., and L. Alexander. 1980. "Factors Which Promote School Achievement in Developing Countries: A Review of the Research." In J. Simmons, ed., *The Education Dilemma.* Oxford: Pergamon Press.

Strauss, J. 1986. "Does Better Nutrition Raise Farm Productivity?" *Journal of Political Economy* 94 (2): 297–320.

Strauss, J., P. Gertler, O. Rahman, and K. Fox. 1993. "Gender and Life-Cycle Differentials on Patterns and Determinants of Adult Health." *Journal of Human Resources* 28 (4): 791–837.

Subbarao, K., and L. Raney. 1993. *Social Gains from Female Education.* World Bank Discussion Paper 194. Washington, D.C.

Summers, Lawrence H. 1992. *Investing in All the People: Educating Women in Developing Countries.* EDI Seminar Paper 45. Washington, D.C.: World Bank.

Tilak, Jandhyala B. G. 1989. *Education and Its Relation to Economic Growth, Poverty, and Income Distribution: Past Evidence and Further Analysis.* World Bank Discussion Paper 46. Washington, D.C.

Tinker, Anne, Patricia Daly, Cynthia Green, Helen Saxenian, Rama Lakshminarayanan, and Kirrin Gill. 1994. *Women's Health and Nutrition: Making a Difference.* World Bank Discussion Paper 256. Washington, D.C.

United Nations, Administrative Committee on Coordination, Subcommittee on Nutrition. 1992. *Second Report on the World Nutrition Situation.* New York.

United Nations. 1993. *World Population Prospects, The 1992 Revision.* New York.

UNESCO. 1990. *Compendium of Statistics on Illiteracy.* Paris: Office of Statistics.

———. 1993a. *Trends and Projections of Enrollment by Level of Education, by Age and by Sex, 1960–2025.* Paris.

———. 1993b. *World Education Report.* Paris.

United Nations Population Fund (UNPFA). 1994. *Note on the Resource Requirements for Population Programmes in the Years 1995–2105.* New York.

Waaler, Hans Th. 1984. "Height, Weight and Mortality: The Norwegian Experience." *Acta Medica Scandinava* 77: 279–303. Suppl. 679, Stockholm.

Weiner, Myron. 1991. *The Child and the State in India.* Princeton, N.J.: Princeton University Press.

Welch, F. 1970. "Education in Production." *Journal of Political Economy* 78: 35–59.

World Bank. 1980. *World Development Report 1980.* New York: Oxford University Press.

———. 1989. "Feeding Latin America's Children." Latin America and the Caribbean Region Report IDP-0049. Washington, D.C.

———. 1990a. *Primary Education.* A World Bank Policy Paper. Washington, D.C.

———. 1990b. *World Development Report 1990: Poverty.* New York: Oxford University Press.

———. 1991a. "Indonesian Education and the World Bank: An Assessment of Two Decades of Lending." Operations Evaluation Department Report 9752. World Bank, Washington, D.C.

———. 1991b. *World Development Report 1991: The Challenge of Development.* New York: Oxford University Press.

———. 1992. *World Development Report 1992: Development and the Environment.* New York: Oxford University Press.

———. 1993a. *The East Asian Miracle: Economic Growth and Public Policy.* A World Bank Policy Research Report. New York: Oxford University Press.

———. 1993b. *Water Resources Management.* A World Bank Policy Study. Washington, D.C.

———. 1993c. *World Development Report 1993: Investing in Health.* New York: Oxford University Press.

———. 1993d. "Human Resources in Latin America and the Caribbean: Priorities and Action." World Bank, Latin America and the Caribbean Region, Washington, D.C.

———. 1994a. *Population and Development: Implications for the World Bank.* World Bank Development in Practice Series. Washington, D.C.

———. 1994b. *Enriching Lives: Overcoming Vitamin and Mineral Malnutrition in Developing Countries.* World Bank Development in Practice Series. Washington, D.C.

———. 1994c. *A New Agenda for Women's Health and Nutrition.* World Bank Development in Practice Series. Washington, D.C.

———. 1995a. *Advancing Social Development.* World Bank, Washington, D.C.

———. 1995b. *Investing in People, The World Bank in Action.* World Bank, Washington, D.C.

———. 1995c. *Priorities and Strategies for Education: A World Bank Review.* Washington, D.C.

Young, M. E. 1994. "Integrated Early Child Development—Challenges and Opportunities." HRO Working Paper 40. World Bank Office of Human Resources Development and Operations Policy, Washington, D.C.

Directions in Development

Begun in 1994, this series contains short essays, written for a general audience, often to summarize published or forthcoming books or to highlight current development issues.

Boom, Crisis, and Adjustment: The Macroeconomic Experience of Developing Countries, 1970–90. A Summary (also available in Spanish)

Financing Health Care in Sub-Saharan Africa through User Fees and Insurance (also available in French)

Investing in People: The World Bank in Action
(also available in French and Spanish)

Meeting the Infrastructure Challenge in Latin America and the Caribbean (also available in Spanish)

MIGA: The First Five Years and Future Challenges

Nurturing Development: Aid and Cooperation in Today's Changing World

Nutrition in Zimbabwe: An Update

Private Sector Participation in Water Supply and Sanitation in Latin America

Reversing the Spiral: The Population, Agriculture, and Environment Nexus in Sub-Saharan Africa (with a separate supplement)

A Strategy for Managing Water in the Middle East and North Africa (also available in Arabic and French)

Unshackling the Private Sector: A Latin American Story

Water Resources Management: A New Policy for a Sustainable Future

Water Supply, Sanitation, and Environmental Sustainability: The Financing Challenge